Handwriting Activity Book

for ages 7-8

This CGP book is bursting with fun activities to build up children's skills and confidence.

It's ideal for extra practice to reinforce what they're learning in primary school. Enjoy!

Handwriting Hints

Here are some tips to help you keep your writing neat:

1. Don't rush. Take your time and concentrate on keeping your writing as tidy as possible.

 2. Make sure that the spaces between words are even.

3. In the first half of this book, use the guidelines to help you keep your letters the same size.

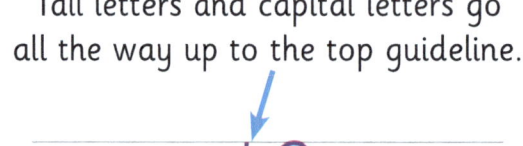

Small letters go between the two middle guidelines.

Tall letters and capital letters go all the way up to the top guideline.

If a letter has a tail, it should go all the way down to the bottom guideline.

 4. When you're writing letters that start with a round shape, move your pen anticlockwise first.

5. Make sure that the round part of a letter is a complete loop — don't leave any gaps.

 6. Make sure the downstrokes of your letters are straight. The downstrokes should all tilt the same amount as well.

7. Remember to go back and dot each i and j, and cross each t when you've finished a word.

8. Don't forget — break letters and capital letters don't join to the letters that come after them. Some schools use different break letters, but in this book they are b, g, j, p, q, s, x, y and z (and you shouldn't join x or z to or from other letters).

> Every school has its own handwriting style. Some schools may form letters and joins differently to how they're written here. Check with the school to see how they write and join each letter.

Contents

The six joins	2
Break letters	6
Capital letters	8
Vowel pairs	10
Consonant pairs	12
Puzzle: Where am I?	14
Writing without guidelines	16
Prefixes	18
Suffixes	20
Safari haikus	22
Pen pals	24
Mermaid instructions	26
A spooky story	28
Answers	30

Published by CGP

Editors:
Andy Cashmore, Helen Clements,
Rachel Craig-McFeely, Becca Lakin

With thanks to Alison Griffin and
Catherine Heygate for the proofreading.

With thanks to Alice Dent
for the copyright research.

ISBN: 978 1 83774 041 3

Printed by Elanders Ltd, Newcastle upon Tyne.
Graphics used on the cover and throughout the book
© Educlips 2023
Cover design concept by emc design ltd.

Text, design, layout and original illustrations
© Coordination Group Publications Ltd. (CGP) 2023
All rights reserved.

Photocopying this book is not permitted, even if you have a CLA licence.
Extra copies are available from CGP with next day delivery • 0800 1712 712 • www.cgpbooks.co.uk

The six joins

How It Works

There are six different ways of joining letters.
Here are the first three joins:

ir

The first join goes from the bottom of a letter to a small letter.

af

The second join goes from the bottom of a letter to a tall letter.

ng

The third join goes from the bottom of a letter to a round letter.

Now Try These

1. Practise the first three joins by copying each pair of letters four times.

   em   ar

   it   el

   us   nd

2. Can you copy these words to label the picture?

eating, checks, cup, cakes, child, meal

3. Now copy the phrases below to practise the first three joins.

 *cheddar and chutney*

little lettuce leaf

chilled iced tea

 *hummus and a nice dip*

lime cut in half

chicken and ham

An Extra Challenge

Pst! May has given you a secret message about her picnic, but the message is written in mirror writing. Can you rewrite the words the right way round to find out what happened at the picnic? Make sure you use joined up writing.

*my dad ate all the cake and
my mum tucked into the tuna*

Pst! You can use a mirror to help you.

Was that as easy as pie?
Tick a box to show how you did.

The six joins

How It Works

Enjoying practising joins? It's time to try joins four to six.

       rv   *wl*   *oq*

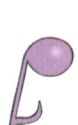

The fourth join goes from the top of a letter to a small letter.

The fifth join goes from the top of a letter to a tall letter.

The sixth join goes from the top of a letter to a round letter.

Now Try These

1. Have a go at joins four to six by copying these letters four times each.

   on   *fi*

   rt   *ok*

   va   *wd*

2. Now try copying out these words.

viola      *clarinet*      *maracas*   

   *conductor*    *note*    *recorder*

3. Copy out these phrases to master your technique.

rock and roll

wonderful concert

lovely melody

terrific voice

having fun with friends

wooden violin

very loud cornet

An Extra Challenge

Oh no! The labels of the musical instruments have been scrambled up.
Can you unscramble each group of letters to make the name of an instrument?
Write the names out on the lines under each label, using joined up writing.

rudms

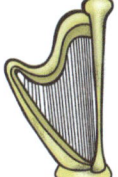

leuft

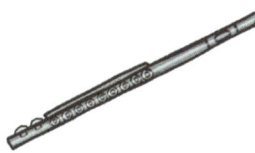

nohr

hrpa

Now, draw lines to match the labels to the correct instruments.

Do you rock at joining letters?
Tick a box to show how you did.

5

Break letters

How It Works

Break letters are letters that don't join to the letter that comes after them. The break letters are:

b g j p q

s y x z ← x and z don't join to the letters that come before them either.

Now Try These

1. These words all start with a break letter. Copy them out.

   gloves      plant

   soil   bird   jug

2. Now copy out these words, which all have at least one break letter in the middle.

   hose   digging   squash   buzzing

   bushes   pumpkins   treehouse

      project

3. Can you copy out the phrases? Keep an eye out for break letters.

sixteen big seeds

the amazing gnome

enjoying the sun

vegetable patch

squeaky wheelbarrow

window boxes

potting plants

An Extra Challenge

Reese has written a list of some things she can see in her garden, but she's forgotten to use spaces. Can you rewrite the phrases on a piece of paper, adding spaces in the right places? Look out for break letters.

thebrightyellowpetals
ashedofgardeningequipment
somecabbageandparsnipseeds

How did that grow? Put a tick in a box to show how you did.

Capital letters

How It Works

Great work so far! You've made it through all six joins and the break letters. Next up are capital letters.

Capital letters never join to other letters.

Lucia   York   January

Now Try These

1. Year 3 are talking about their birthdays.
   Copy out the names of the children.

   Haider   *Maisie*

   Dave   *Jenny*

   Priya   *William*

2. The children are making a calendar so that they remember each other's birthdays. Can you copy out the months that they were born in?

   March    *June*    *May*    *July*

      *January*    *September*

3. Now the class are sharing their plans for their birthdays. Copy out the phrases for some more practice.

football with Isaac   *lunch in Cardiff*

shopping in Leeds   *eating cake with Annie*

seeing friends on Saturday

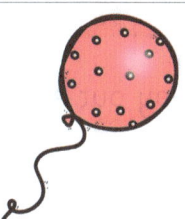

a day at Pimbury Zoo

An Extra Challenge

Uh-oh! Freya has written an invitation to her birthday party, but she has forgotten to use capital letters! Can you rewrite the invitation, adding capital letters where they are needed? Remember — capitals never join to other letters.

dear akio,

will you come to my party?
it is on sunday 11th april in oxford.

from freya

Do you feel like celebrating? Put a tick in one of the boxes.

Vowel pairs

How It Works

Vowel pairs appear in lots of words, so it's important to practise them.

ou   ei   ai   ue

Now Try These

1. Copy out each vowel pair four times.

   ua _____   ee _____

   oi _____   ia _____

   ea _____   io _____

2. Now copy out the words containing vowel pairs to label the scene below.

   moon   clouds   fairy

                             moat

   tree

                             shield

   giant

         armour

3. Now try copying out these phrases.

their violet outfit

the pearl tiara

broom for sweeping

4. Have a go at copying out these sentences.

The greedy heir counted their coins.

A heroic soldier rescued the maiden.

An Extra Challenge

Nora has received a note from Prince Cai, but some of the words are missing. Can you help her decode the message by writing the words from the box in the right spaces? Then, copy the note onto a piece of paper in joined up handwriting.

It would be an _____ to take you to the ball. Please _____ me by the _____ in the wood and wear a hooded _____ .

clearing
cloak
honour
meet

How did you find it? Were these vowel pairs magical? Tick a box.

Consonant pairs

How It Works

You can find consonant pairs in lots of words. It's important to practise writing them.

Now Try These

1. Copy each consonant pair four times.

   ck   wh

    wr   fl

   nd   ch

   ph   th

2. Now try copying each of the words containing consonant pairs below.

   stand      chair   theatre   ticket

   photographer      flowers

3. Can you copy these phrases onto the lines?

   flashes everywhere   *hundreds of autographs*

   the main character

4. Copy out the sentences.

   She found watching the film dull.

   The actor cheered when he won.

An Extra Challenge

Ruth accidentally added some extra letters when she was writing her diary entry. Circle the extra letters and then rewrite the sentences without them.

   *I listtened to the sooundtrack.*
I pput on myy whhite drress.

Can you make a word using the extra letters you circled? Write it here: _____

Was that an award-winning performance? Tick a box.

Where am I?

Taylor is hiding somewhere in the park and they've left you some clues about their hiding place. Can you work out where they are hiding? Answer each clue using your best joined up handwriting, then use your answers to reveal Taylor's location.

Clue 1 — This sentence has been written backwards. Can you rewrite the sentence so it's the right way round?

.tiq bnas eht ekil I

_____

Circle the third word in the sentence.

Clue 2 — Can you rewrite this sentence on the line, adding in spaces where needed?

Thetwoduckslookatme.

_____

Circle the fourth word in the sentence.

Clue 3 — Rearrange the words in the box to make a sentence. Write the sentence on the lines below.

sat   the   bench   boy
on   The   wooden

_____

_____

Circle the word in the sentence that has a suffix.

14

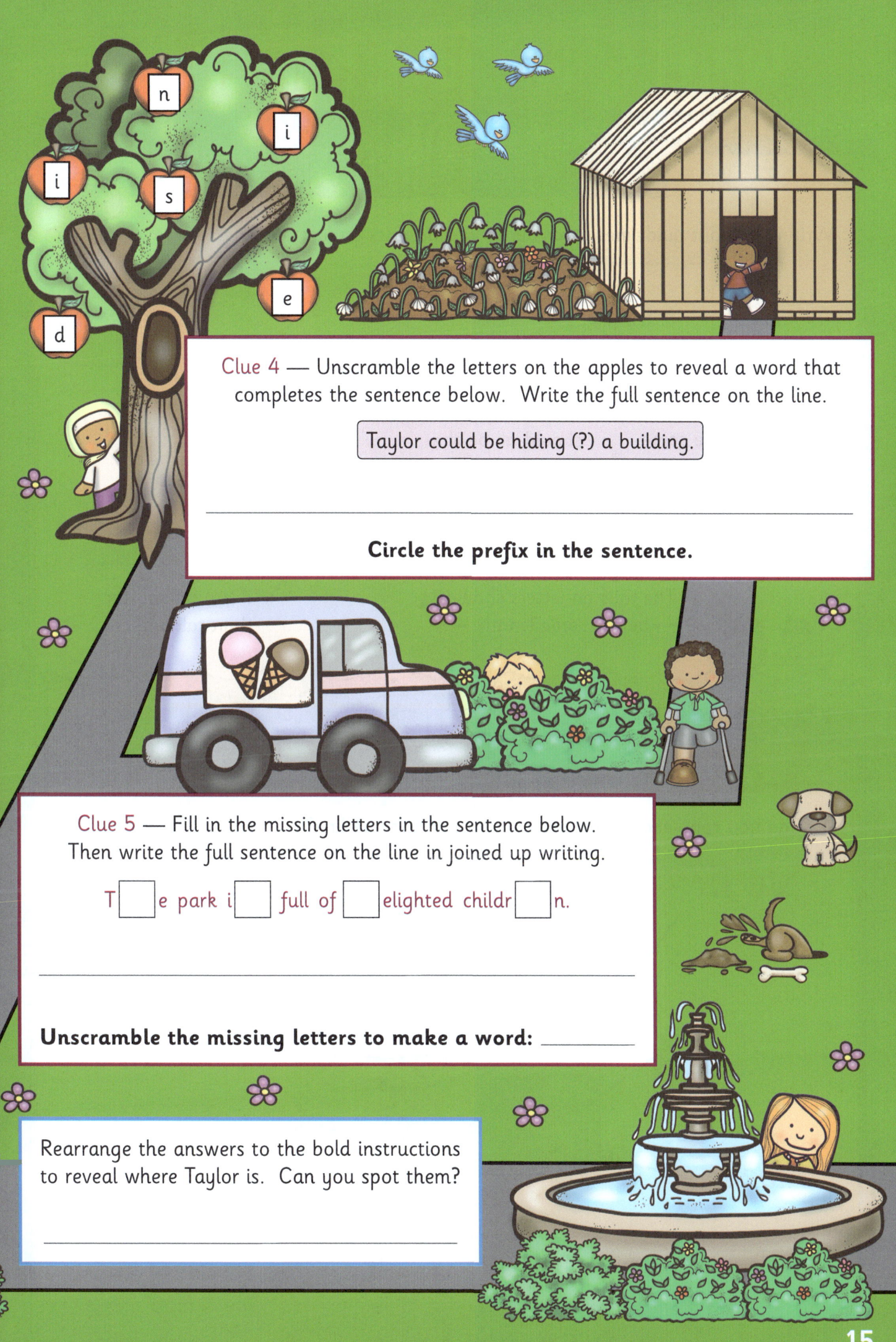

Clue 4 — Unscramble the letters on the apples to reveal a word that completes the sentence below. Write the full sentence on the line.

Taylor could be hiding (?) a building.

_____

Circle the prefix in the sentence.

Clue 5 — Fill in the missing letters in the sentence below. Then write the full sentence on the line in joined up writing.

T☐e park i☐ full of ☐elighted childr☐n.

_____

Unscramble the missing letters to make a word: _____

Rearrange the answers to the bold instructions to reveal where Taylor is. Can you spot them?

_____

Writing without guidelines

How It Works

Writing without guidelines means your writing rests on just one line.

hiking → *hiking*

Here are some things to remember when writing without guidelines:

Capital letters should be the same size as tall letters.

Small letters should all be the same height.

Tall letters should all be the same height.

They're rowing on the lake.

The tails on letters should be the same length.

't' is a bit shorter than tall letters.

Now Try These

1. Can you copy each of the words out onto just one line?

ducks   *forest*   *nature*

light   *kayak*

pegs   *guitar*

boots

2. Copy out each of these phrases twice.

   twit twoo _____

   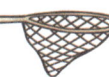 *fishing net* _____

   a bike ride _____

    *ghost stories* _____

3. Can you copy the sentences out neatly on the lines below? Remember — capitals and tall letters should be the same height.

   Use your binoculars to spot birds.

   _____

   He cooks sausages on the campfire.

   _____

An Extra Challenge

Pablo needs to copy the checklist for his summer camping trip from the poster below. Can you copy out the items in the list onto the lines in joined up writing, to show him how to write the words neatly?

 **Kit List**

You will need to bring:
- Waterproof jacket
- Sleeping bag and tent
- Torch and spare battery
- Comfortable shoes
- Your favourite snacks

Did these pages guide you towards success? Tick a box.

Prefixes

How It Works

A prefix is a group of letters that goes at the beginning of a word to make a new word.

un ➕ aware ➡ unaware

↑ prefix ↑ word ↑ new word

Remember to join up the prefix to the new word, unless the prefix ends in a break letter.

Now Try These

1. Copy out each of these common prefixes twice on the lines below.

   un   sub   anti

   re   dis   super

2. Copy the prefix in the box onto the first line using joined up writing.
   Then, add the prefix to the green word and write the new word on the second line.

   il ➡ ____ + legal ➡ _____
   sub ➡ ____ + merge ➡ _____
   mis ➡ ____ + behave ➡ _____

3. These words all start with a prefix. Copy them out on the lines below.

   disobey   anticlockwise   recycle

   mistake   unfriendly   inactive

4. Can you copy the sentences out neatly on the lines below?

My kitten refused to play with the submarine.

There is an antisocial bird by the supermarket.

An unlucky rabbit knocked the superglue over.

The irresponsible pet removed the petals.

An Extra Challenge

Jeremy is feeling upset. Can you find out why? Write the words from the pink box in the right gaps in the speech bubble. Make sure you use joined up writing.

I have _____ my pink socks.
It seems like they have _____ !
Finding them will be _____ .
I'm _____ to walk Rufus now.

unable   misplaced   impossible   disappeared

Now copy out Jeremy's explanation on a piece of paper.

Was this page of prefixes perfect? Give a box a tick.

Suffixes

How It Works

A suffix is a group of letters that is added to the end of a word to make a new word. Sometimes the spelling of the original word changes when the suffix is added.

sweet ➕ er ➡ sweeter

↑ word   ↑ suffix   ↑ new word

Unless the word ends in a break letter, join the word and suffix together.

Now Try These

1. Copy out each suffix twice on the lines below.

   ing _____ _ly_ _____ _ed_ _____

   ful _____ _en_ _____ _er_ _____

   ous _____ _ation_ _____

2. Each of these words ends with a suffix.
   Can you copy them out on the lines below?

   restless _____   _furious_ _____   _hopeful_ _____

   hotter _____   _playing_ _____   _bitten_ _____

   calmly _____   _excitement_ _____

3. Copy out the phrases containing suffixes.

　　laziness and relaxation　　　　swimming quickly

4. Can you circle the suffixes in the sentences below? Then copy out the sentences.

　　She applied her sun cream correctly.

　　It was much cooler in the shaded area.

　　They were building an enormous sandcastle.

An Extra Challenge

A message has washed up on the shore, but a seagull has eaten all the suffixes! Can you use the suffixes in the green boxes to complete the half-eaten words? Write the completed words on the lines. Then, copy the note onto a piece of paper.

I am stay☐ on a peace☐ island full of friend☐ seals. I think one even wav☐ at me. What a joy☐ holiday!

| ful |
| ous |
| ed |
| ly |
| ing |

Do you think suffixes are sensational? Tick a box.

Safari haikus

How It Works

Excellent work so far! You've made some great progress with handwriting. It's time to put your skills to the test with these four animal haikus.

A haiku is a type of poem which has three lines. It has five syllables in the first and third lines and seven syllables in the second line.

Now Try These

1. Copy out these haikus one line at a time.

   Elegant giant

   Strides gracefully through the grass

   Its neck in the clouds.

   King of the jungle

   Impressive mane and sharp teeth

   Hear its roar and run.

2. Can you copy the haikus onto the lines below?

A trumpeting trunk
And enormous ears flapping
Watch out for its tusks.

_____

_____

_____

Beware this creature
Spotted coat and harmful bite
Laughing endlessly.

_____

_____

_____

An Extra Challenge

Bradley wrote his own haiku while on safari, but all the lines are mixed up.
Use the information about haikus on the previous page to put them in the right order.
Then, copy the haiku onto a separate piece of paper in your neatest writing.

Not a horse or a donkey

Running with its herd.

Stripy and speedy

Can you guess which safari animal this poem is about?

How did it go? Are you wild about handwriting? Tick a box.

Pen pals

How It Works

You're making terrific progress with longer pieces of writing.

Time to test your handwriting skills with these letters between friends.

Now Try These

1. Jorge is writing a letter to his friend Caroline. Can you copy out his letter one line at a time?

 Dear Caroline,

 It was lovely to hear from you recently.

 Your new house sounds absolutely amazing!

 *I can't wait to visit you in a few weeks' time.*

 How is your new school? Have you made

 *lots of friends? We miss you in Year 3.*

 *From Jorge*

2. Caroline has replied to Jorge's letter. Can you copy what she wrote on the lines?

Dear Jorge,
Everyone at my new school is so nice.
Moving wasn't as scary as I thought.
I can't wait to show you around during half term. We will have the best time!
From Caroline

An Extra Challenge

Jorge wrote to Caroline to thank her for letting him visit, but his dog ate the letter! Can you copy out the remains of Jorge's letter in your neatest joined up writing? Then write the rest of the letter, using the information in the speech bubble.

Dear Caroline,

Thank you for letting me stay with you during half term. I had so much fun.

We went bowling and ate ice cream.

Did you put your stamp on these pages? Put a tick in a box.

Mermaid instructions

How It Works

You've done some great work so far — only a few more pages left to go.

Put everything you've learnt into practice by copying the instructions on this page as neatly as possible.

Now Try This

1. These instructions tell you the ten steps for making friends with a mermaid. Copy the instructions onto the lines on the next page.

   1. Find a quiet beach where you can't be seen.
   2. Collect three or four beautiful shells.
   3. Sit as close to the water as you can.
   4. Put the largest shell to your lips.
   5. Blow into it and play a soft tune.
   6. Watch as a mermaid appears.
   7. Give them your remaining shells.
   8. If they offer you some seaweed, accept it.
   9. Wave as they disappear into the water.
   10. Make a wish that you will see them again.

_____

_____

_____

_____

_____

_____

_____

_____

_____

_____

An Extra Challenge

Olufemi has written some instructions for a new swimming technique, but he has forgotten to use spaces. Can you rewrite the instructions, adding spaces in the right places?

1. Keepyourarmsbyyoursides.
2. Moveyourtailupanddownslowly.
3. Don'tforgettowatchoutforsharks.

Did that go swimmingly?
Put a tick in one of the boxes.

A spooky story

How It Works

Congratulations! You're becoming a real handwriting pro.

This spooky story is the last bit of handwriting practice.

Now Try These

1. Read the opening of this scary story.
   Then copy it out onto the lines below.

   Ghadir froze when she entered the house. She was surrounded by dusty cobwebs and there was a chill in the air. Ghadir felt like someone was watching her. Suddenly, a loud noise came from the study. She tiptoed cautiously towards the sound to find out what it was...

2. Now copy out the next part of the story.

Ghadir trembled with fear as she approached the door. Closing her eyes, she reached for the handle and pushed. A tall, dark figure was waiting for her in the corner of the room. She screamed, then breathed a sigh of relief when she realised it was only a coat stand.

An Extra Challenge

These two scenes show what happens next in the scary story.

Can you use them to help you write an ending to the story?

Make sure you use your best handwriting.

How did it go? Are you feeling fearless about handwriting?

Answers

Here are the answers to the Extra Challenges and the puzzle. All answers should be written in joined up writing.

Pages 2-3 — The six joins

my dad ate all the cake and my mum tucked into the tuna

Pages 4-5 — The six joins

drums

flute

horn

harp

Pages 6-7 — Break letters

the bright yellow petals
a shed of gardening equipment
some cabbage and parsnip seeds

Pages 8-9 — Capital letters

Dear Akio,
Will you come to my party?
It is on Sunday 11th April in Oxford.
From Freya

Pages 10-11 — Vowel pairs

It would be an honour to take you to the ball. Please meet me by the clearing in the wood and wear a hooded cloak.

Pages 12-13 — Consonant pairs

I listened to the soundtrack. I put on my white dress.

The word 'trophy' can be made using the extra letters.

Pages 14-15 — Where am I?

1. I like the sandpit. — **the**
2. The two ducks look at me. — **look**
3. The boy sat on the wooden bench. — **wooden**
4. Taylor could be hiding inside a building. — **in**
5. The park is full of delighted children. — **shed**

Taylor's location: Look in the wooden shed.

Pages 16-17 — Writing without guidelines

You should have written the equipment list neatly on the guidelines in joined up writing.

Pages 18-19 — Prefixes

I have misplaced my pink socks.
It seems like they have disappeared!
Finding them will be impossible.
I'm unable to walk Rufus now.

Pages 20-21 — Suffixes

staying, peaceful, friendly, waved, joyous

I am staying on a peaceful island full of friendly seals. I think one even waved at me. What a joyous holiday!

Pages 22-23 — Safari haikus

Stripy and speedy
Not a horse or a donkey
Running with its herd.

The haiku is about a zebra.

Pages 24-25 — Pen pals

Any sensible ending to the letter. You can refer to bowling and eating ice cream, or use your own ideas.

Pages 26-27 — Mermaid instructions

1. Keep your arms by your sides.
2. Move your tail up and down slowly.
3. Don't forget to watch out for sharks.

Pages 28-29 — A spooky story

You should have written an ending where the noise turns out to be Ghadir's friend Felix trying to scare her by dressing up as a ghost.